HOW TO PLAN YOUR WEDDING AND STAY SANE!

25 Tips For Making Sure You & Your Partner Plan This Whole Shebang *TOGETHER*

By
JP Reynolds, M.Div.

We are all a little weird and life's a little weird

And when we find someone whose weirdness is compatible with ours

We join up with them and fall in mutual weirdness and call it love.

Robert Fulghum

TABLE OF CONTENTS

INTRODUCTION

Why This Book?

true story

I was at a Starbucks jotting down ideas for this book when, by chance, I met up with Meredith, a bride whose wedding I officiated several years ago. Everything that could have gone wrong with her wedding did. And by "everything" I'm not exaggerating.

The florist had mixed-up the flowers for her bouquet. The tablecloths were black and in her culture black symbolized death. The musicians were late. The shuttle van from the hotel broke down and guests were stranded for half an hour. Shortly before the ceremony, the zipper on her dress broke. The ceremony was delayed more than an hour.

Through it all she remained calm. Not once did she get angry. I was in awe of her and now, finally, I could ask how she did it. She said, "It was the happiest day of my life and Patrick (groom) and I had decided that we wouldn't let anything ruin our happiness."

It was that simple.

She told me that the ceremony was beautiful (thank you!) and that she and Patrick and their guests had a blast at the reception, despite mixed-up flowers and linens. The months leading up to the wedding had their own stress beginning with her dad pressuring them to get married in the Catholic Church. Since she and Patrick are not regular churchgoers, she thought it'd be hypocritical. Still, her father tried to do a guilt trip on her. Oh, and her father was divorced twice and married three times!

Her mother told her that she didn't want anything to do with her ex-husband's third wife and didn't want the woman sitting in the front row even though Meredith's dad was paying for the wedding. The mother was friends with the second wife and wanted that woman to sit next to her in the front row even though Meredith's dad and this woman were no longer on speaking terms.

A few weeks before their wedding, at our last meeting, when I asked them how they were doing, I remember Patrick saying: "Well, we're learning to say 'I'm sorry' to each other a lot faster than we used to."

We laughed, BUT he did speak to an important issue – communication.

Patrick recognized that the only way he and Meredith could protect and keep each other sane was by making time to talk with each other while planning for their wedding.

It's because they had such a clear vision of their wedding, a vision that came from months of honest conversation, that no mishap, however surprising or annoying, was able to ruin the magic of their dream day.

Over the years I've seen the startling difference between couples who communicate with trust and confidence and those who are stuck in a rut of complaining and accusing. The former celebrate their wedding day with sparkling eyes while the later struggle just to survive the day.

I'm convinced that you'll outwit the wackiness and inevitable frustrations of your wedding planning only if you and your partner talk with each other – in ways that are healthy and honest.

At this point in your relationship, you've developed routines, "dance steps," for communicating with each other. Are these routines letting you get heard and helping you get your needs taken seriously OR are they causing confusion and hurt?

This book offers you tips, tricks and techniques for communicating in ways that will help you:

- Resist pressure from family and friends so you make decisions that honor and reflect you and your partner.
- Express your emotions without saddling guilt trips on each other.
- Argue fairly so you don't drive each other crazy.
- Listen so you can both be on the same page.
- Sit down and talk about the issues you've been avoiding.
- Look at challenges from each other's P.O.V. so you can solve seemingly unsolvable problems.

Each time you turn to this book I hope you find a chapter that makes you smile in recognition, sigh with relief and assure you that you and your partner can protect each other from the wackiness of wedding planning so as together keep your "I" in your "I Do!"

TIP 1

Reality Isn't Always True!

true story

Two weeks after my ordination I officiated my first wedding. Beyond nervous, I was sweating and not just because it was a scorching New York June afternoon. I got to the church early to make sure the sacristan turned on the air conditioner (the church windows were sealed).

The church was packed – both the bride and groom were Italian and came from big families. Because it was a church service, the ceremony was slated to last about 45 minutes. I'd rehearsed everything in my head at least a dozen times. I was anxious, but excited – this is what I had prepared so many years for.

Twenty minutes into the ceremony, I was dripping sweat under my robes. I noticed that family and guests were shifting in their seats. The bride and groom looked antsy.

I panicked. I was convinced that I was boring everyone! And so I talked faster. With sweat pouring out of me, I decided to skip a reading; I cut out some prayers.

Finally, I zapped them with a blessing and pronounced them husband and wife.

Afterwards I hurried back to the sacristy and there found the sacristan embarrassed and apologetic. Turns out, he switched on the heat instead of the air conditioner. It was a humid 90 degrees out and we all were trapped in a church that was blasting heat!

All through the ceremony, I thought I was sweating because I was nervous. I thought the guests were restless because they were bored. Instead, we were all just ready to pass out from the heat. Later, at the reception, folks laughed and thanked me for having enough sense to cut things short.

This wacky story illustrates THE great truth I urge you to keep in mind:

What we think influences what we feel

AND

What we feel influences what we think.

Sanity Saver Questions ~

- What are you telling yourself in terms of how you should and should not feel as you plan your wedding?
- Where do these beliefs come from?
- Are those feelings helping you navigate the stress of planning or are they adding to it?

Emotions are neither "good" nor "bad." However –

Emotions either allow us to react to people and situations in a healthy way OR they trip us up and cause us to sabotage our relationships and plans.

Emotions that prevent us from acting in our own best interest are grounded in some very irrational thoughts –lies – that we play so often in our heads we're not even aware of them.

There are Four Lies in particular that can cause you to stress out while planning your wedding.

4 Most Common Crazy-Making Lies A Couple Can Buy Into

1. You believe that everything must be perfect in order to be good.
2. You believe that your wedding should involve certain people and elements no matter how uncomfortable they make you and your partner feel.
3. You believe that there are aspects of the wedding planning that you cannot control and that you must give in to.
4. You believe that you – and you alone – cause the feelings your family and friends experience during the long process of planning your wedding.

Buy into one or more of these lies and you're destined for MASSIVE headaches.

Read on as I review each of these lies with you.

TIP 2

Perfection Is For Masochists

true story

I spoke with Miriam three days before her wedding; she was in tears from exhaustion. It was a garden ceremony and she was tying purple ribbons around one hundred and fifty hand fans that would also serve as programs.

When I asked why she was adding the ribbons, she explained that the purple would match her bridesmaids' dresses and it was the main color theme. I asked if she had any friends who could help her tie the ribbons. She said she didn't want to bother anyone.

When I told her that five years after the wedding few if any will remember the purple ribbons, she looked annoyed and said the fateful words: "But I want everything to be perfect."

Stop! Obsessive devotion to perfection will cause you to lose your sanity!

Here is the first crazy-making lie that couples play in their heads:

Everything must be PERFECT in order for it to be good.

Sanity Saver Questions ~

- Do you and your partner have the same idea of "perfection?"

- What is the price you're willing to pay for perfection?

- Do you know just how much a price you're going to pay for "perfection"?

Remember:

Your wedding day is bigger than ribbons – and ring pillows and place cards and running make-up!

TIP 3

You Shouldn't Cling To 'Should'

true story

It was an outdoor wedding. Argentina and Marco (30's) had been together for more than five years and were great partners. Towards the end of their ceremony Argentina's mother suddenly stood up and walked towards me.

I was puzzled, but then remembered she was a widow. Maybe she wanted to thank folks for coming. Maybe she was supposed to read a poem and they forgot to tell me.

I walked over to her and in a voice only I could hear, she said these immortal words: *"Do not pronounce them husband and wife, I have reservations."*

I was beyond stunned. I thought, "Sweetheart, do you really think I'm going to hand over my mic so we can enjoy a Jerry Springer moment?"

I smiled and said to her: *"The only reservation you better have is for dinner."* Hey, I grew up in the Bronx!

I raced back to the couple and pronounced them husband & wife. In fact, I've never pronounced a couple husband & wife as quickly as that couple.

As soon as the ceremony was over, I was swarmed by the photographer, videographer, musicians and coordinator. No one could believe what had happened.

But I was concerned about Argentina. As I gave her a hug, she told me something I think of every time I meet with a couple. She said: ***"I guess I forgot to tell you about my mother."***

Everyone knew that momma was "unpredictable." Everyone knew that momma was not happy with the marriage. And everyone told Argentina not to invite momma.

And Argentina?

She knew her mother was unpredictable, but, out of guilt, she felt she "should" invite her. She invited her, knowing that her mother may attempt to disrupt the joy of her day.

Throughout the morning and leading up to the ceremony, Argentina was on the proverbial pins-n-needles. Throughout the ceremony many of her guests were apprehensive. All because her mother held the day hostage.

Argentina and Marco got into many arguments over her mother. And, yes, I think I detected an "I told you so" smirk in Marco's eyes!

Here is the second crazy-making lie couples play in their heads:

There are things they should do in their wedding
because that's how things should be.

Don't plan your wedding out of a sense of should!

Plan it out of a sense of what you and your partner want to do.

Be guided by what reflects you as a couple.

Sanity Saver Questions ~

- Are there any decisions you've made out of guilt rather than desire?

- Are you and your partner ready to live with the outcomes of those decisions?

- What is the worst thing that could happen if you refused to be influenced by "guilt"?

Remember:

No one – no friend, no family member – has the right to take your day hostage by selfish whims and desires.

TIP 4

You Always Have A Choice

true story

Rita and Peter were getting married at a 5-star resort in Southern California. They didn't have a budget because they didn't need one. Rita's parents were divorced and her wealthy father was footing the bill for everything. One catch – if she invited her mother, he wouldn't pay for the wedding.

Rita wanted a fabulous wedding that would blow people away but since her father was paying for it all, what could she do? Her father put her in a seemingly hopeless situation. So, she caved and didn't invite her mother.

Actually, though, he didn't put her in a hopeless position. Rita had a choice and she chose to compromise. To lessen her guilt, she chose to believe she was caught in a hopeless predicament.

Rita needlessly complicated her life by feeling helpless. Of course, she then took her frustrations out on her hapless groom!

What Rita failed to accept was that she freely made a decision. Wrong or right, nice or not, she needed to own her choice and not blame her father.

Here is the third lie that couples play in their heads:

When it comes to the essential aspects of their wedding, they don't always have a choice.

So often when we say, "I can't" what we're really saying is, "I don't want to."

There are many aspects to a wedding where it's just "easier" to let mom or dad have their way. And that's fine. But when it comes to the fundamental aspects of the celebration, you and your partner do have choices.

Sanity Saver Questions ~

- Where in the planning do you feel helpless?

- Are you really helpless or is it that you don't want to make hard decisions?

- What would happen if you let go of blaming others and just accepted responsibility for your choices, even if people object to those choices?

Remember:

If you choose to go along with family's desires that go counter to your own, then you don't have the right to complain. By not speaking up, you are agreeing.

TIP 5

Take A Deep Sigh – Someone Will Feel Hurt By You!

true story

Gloria and Sal, a couple in their mid-thirties, hired me to officiate their ceremony at an estate in Santa Barbara. They each had been raised Catholic, but over the years drifted away. They went to Midnight Christmas mass and that pretty much was it.

Both sets of parents were practicing Catholics and they knew that the couple no longer practiced the religion. Although knowing that, both sets of parents told them that if they didn't get married in the church, they wouldn't attend the wedding.

At first, Gloria and Sal resisted and then, just a month after hiring me, caved in. They told me that they didn't want to hurt their parents' feelings.

They decided to focus on the reception and after-party. Of course, their parents had much to say about that as well since they were jointly paying for it. Eventually, Gloria and Sal just wanted to get their wedding over with so they could get on with their lives.

Here is the fourth lie that couples play in their heads:

They and they alone are ultimately responsible for the happiness of their families and friends on the day of their wedding.

Let me be very clear: No one has the right to emotionally blackmail you. No one has the right to throw ultimatums your way. Family and friends can choose to honor your life and your decisions, or they can choose to place the burden of how they feel upon you and your partner.

If they choose the later, then that's not love. It's emotional blackmail. The truth is – more times than not, you are not responsible for other people's feelings.

We are each responsible for our own feelings – and the choices we make based on those feelings.

Brides and grooms often tell me of the compromises they've made so as to "make peace." That's fine, so long as you remember – this is your wedding. I know that a wedding is not only about the couple; it's also about the families. However, a wedding really doesn't celebrate the union of two families. Your parents aren't going to be sharing a bed together! A wedding celebrates the union of two people – you and your partner.

Sanity Saver Questions ~

- Where in the planning are you and your partner willing to compromise?

- Where are you and your partner not willing to compromise?

- Are you on the same page, right now, today?

Remember:

When you "make peace" make sure you're remaining true to you and your partner. Otherwise, you will have no peace. A shared vision is your compass, as it will help you not let others' emotions swamp you.

TIP 6

Feelings Will Drive You Nuts

true story

Maureen's maid of honor, Denise, was driving down from San Francisco to Hollywood for the weekend. They were going to work on wedding stuff. Denise said she'd be there in time for dinner.

6:00pm – no maid of honor. A couple of hours passed – no maid of honor and no phone call. By 11:00pm Maureen was panicked as she hadn't been able to get hold of Denise. At 11:30pm Denise breezed in, much to Maureen's relief. But when Maureen asked what had happened, Denise lamely said that she'd gotten a "late" start. She went on to say that her phone battery died. Maureen was dumfounded that Denise hadn't given any thought to how worried she'd be.

Maureen admitted that she yelled at Denise, demanding to know what was wrong with her that she couldn't have stopped to call. And, of course, Denise grew annoyed with Maureen for "making a big deal out of nothing." Maureen shot back that she now wondered why she'd asked her to be her maid of honor. Denise wasn't going to have any of that and hit back with the zinger, "I've got more on my mind than just your wedding."

There were more nasty words and then silence. Come morning, both women apologized and then spent the rest of the weekend trying to repair the damage.

Emotions – ugh! Buttons are pressed quickly. Words spit themselves out easily. And the tone of it all is often biting, sarcastic and condescending. And that's when you're not planning a wedding!

Here's the reality: feelings get jumbled-up very easily.

Often times while we feel one strong emotion, there's another secondary emotion(s), lurking around. At times it's difficult for us to figure out how best to express what we're feeling. And so we end up expressing what is the strongest of the feelings.

Although Maureen was relieved Denise was safe, her annoyance was the stronger feeling and that's what came out in her tone and words. Then the conversation quickly took on a life of its own that wasn't pretty.

More times than not, we don't reveal the complexity of what we're feeling. During planning, your emotions will get jumbled and will be hard to sort out. The "trick" is to recognize what you're feeling and make that mindful effort to explain to your partner, friend, parent or vendor what's going on inside your head and heart.

And, yes, that requires trust and honesty. Do you and your partner have that "dance step" in place?

Sanity Saver Questions ~

- In the past week, has you're partner asked how you're feeling?

- Have you been able to give your partner some insight into what you're feeling?

- In the past week have you been able to tune in to your partner's feelings?

Remember:

It's fine to feel what you feel, but you have to let your partner (or friend, sibling, parent) understand the complexity of what you're feeling. Otherwise, you'll just come off as some crazy person to be avoided!

Tip 7

True Kindness Is the Only Kind Of Kind

true story

I recently reunited with a couple whose wedding I officiated fifteen years ago. They look older but their spirits are as I remember them. Open, inquisitive and clearly defined in their ongoing aspirations. "Jack Daniels" joined us at the table and story begat story. It was a magical night.

As I was leaving, Frank suddenly asked me, "Do you know why Renee and I are still in love?" Various answers came to mind, but I just said, "No, why are you still in love?" With pride he replied, "We're kind to each other."

Frank explained how he and Renee consciously decided that they didn't ever want to lose sight of being each other's partner and best friend – not punching bag or dumping ground for the day's irritations. So simple, yet so challenging!

No matter how strong and healthy your relationship, stress cracks will appear when the bliss of engagement turns into the craziness of actual planning. Planning your wedding will test your kindness to each other in surprising ways.

While there are many ways in which to be kind to your partner, how you express what you're feeling is one of the most important. Letting your partner know how you feel in a way that doesn't turn him or her into that punching bag is one of the kindest things you can do – for your partner and each other.

4 Things To Avoid When Expressing Your Feelings!

1. Has anyone ever been annoyed with you and sarcastically asked (yelled) *"What the #@%^ is wrong with you?"* And when they asked what's wrong with you, did you smile, sit down and tell them what's wrong with you? Didn't think so!

Loudly attacking someone with phrases such as, *"What's wrong with you?" "Leave me alone – can't you see I'm busy?"* or *"You're driving me nuts!"* will definitely drive the other person away. The only problem is they'll be so annoyed with you that they won't want to talk to you later on or help you. And really, why should they?

Avoid outbursts. They just signal that you're in a bad mood without offering any insight into why. There's never a good time to be nasty!

2. Do you end heated discussions with, *"That's just how I am"*? Nice. Cute. Useless! No one is ever "just" something. We always feel a certain way for a reason. If you don't tell the other person why you're feeling what you're feeling, they'll storm off thinking that you're a jerk (or some stronger word).

Avoid dramatic declarations. They provide no clue as to why you are the way you "just" are and most likely your partner is going to feel "just" fed up with you for stonewalling him or her.

3. What about when you say, *"I'm kinda mad at you right now."* How mad is "kinda"? Is your "kinda" the same as your partner's "kinda"? Understated expressions can only confuse your partner. The clearer you are in describing how you feel, the better chance your partner has of understanding you and being able to help you.

Avoid vague words such as, *almost, better, big, cheap, easy, expensive, in a minute, probably, soon.* You know what you mean by these words, but your partner may not. When you say, *"I'll be ready in a minute,"* how many minutes is that "minute"! You decrease your chances for being misunderstood, the more specific you are.

4. And the single most important word to avoid is: **YOU.** *You never. You always. You disappoint me. You make me sick.*

When you attack the other person with a barrage of "you's" all they can do is one of two things – lash out or become defensive.

At my first meeting with a couple I can easily predict how they'll handle planning stress. If they repeatedly use the phrase *"we're feeling"* then I know they're in this together. But sometimes, couples speak in a sarcastic tone, tossing out *"you this and you that"* at a rapid pace. Clearly, the stress is going to bring them to their knees long before their wedding day.

Avoid saying "you." That one little word has the power to press your partner's buttons. You know how you react when someone attacks you with "you," so why attack your partner with "you" when you know what you're doing!

We're all guilty of what I've just described. Why? Because old habits die hard. Because we're lazy. Because we think we shouldn't have to explain ourselves.

BUT, you do have to explain yourself; otherwise, you'll drive your partner nuts and, in turn, they will drive you nuts!

Sanity Saver Questions ~

- In the past week, how many times have you accused your partner of not "caring"?

- In the past week how many times have you complained to someone about your partner not understanding you?

- In the past week how many times have you understated your feelings or bombarded your partner with "you" accusations?

- What would you like to see happen differently?

Remember:

You protect and keep each other sane when you –

Acknowledge each other's feelings.

Try to understand and not judge those feelings.

Take responsibility for owning and expressing your feelings.

TIP 8

Your Partner Is Not A Mind Reader

As you know, the wedding planning process is laced with stress. And often times stress bubbles up from unrealistic expectations.

Studies have shown that the longer we've known someone, the more we love someone, the more we expect that person to know us so well that we don't have to tell them what we're thinking. As wacky as it sounds, we expect them to be able to read our mind!

When meeting with couples I hear classic phrases such as, "Why do I have to ask him? He should know without me asking." "She said she didn't care. How was I supposed to know that this was a big deal to her?"

In the midst of "should" and "why" and "supposed to" it's vital to remember that your partner is many wonderful things, BUT, he / she is not a mind reader. And even though they can't read your mind, they still do love you!

If you need your partner to know how you're feeling or what you're thinking or needing, let them know. Don't blame; don't accuse. Just tell them.

And if you're not sure what it is your partner is saying, ask for clarification. Admit that you don't understand.

Here are some non-mind-reading phrases:

"I need you to know that_____."

"I'm feeling _____ right now and I need you to_____."

"I want to help and I'm not sure how. What can I do?"

"I'm not sure I understand what you mean when you say_____."

"Are you sure everything is good because you look _____. Are you?"

REMEMBER:

There are many people who will play games with you as you plan for your wedding. Please don't play games with each other.

TIP 9

Figure Out Why You Like Arguing The Way You Do

true story

Lyn and Danny came to me for pre-marital counseling – at Danny's insistence. Lyn was uneasy – everything was fine, so what were they doing seeing me? I explained that my approach is from a communications angle and I don't have a structured format.

Still uneasy, she said they didn't have any problems communicating, though at times she "might" be a bit too passive in their arguments – especially when Danny's his usual "pigheaded" self.

Danny readily admitted that he's competitive and enjoys arguing even when he knows he's wrong.

I asked Lyn if she enjoyed arguing when he was in the "zone." She said it didn't matter because although she hates it, she just shuts down and lets him have his way.

At this point, Danny jumped in saying that he hated when she shuts down. I asked if he heard why she shuts down. *"Yes, but. . ."* and before he could finish, Lyn demanded, *"Then why do you do it? You know I don't want to argue. I just want to get what I want,"* she matter-of-factly explained.

"There, that's the kind of attitude I don't like," said Danny. *"She doesn't take what I say seriously. I'll explain why we need to do something a certain way and she just ignores everything I say."*

"Is that true?" I asked Lyn.

"I know what he's going to say and I don't want to be told I can't have something when I feel I should have it. He doesn't respect me when he doesn't listen to why I want something."

Exasperated, Danny tossed out, *"She doesn't have reasons for anything. All she has are feelings."*

I want to point out that Danny and Lyn were actually very polite in the way they spoke to each other – this was not a shouting match.

However, by dint of personality and profession (engineer) Danny values logic. Lyn, by dint of personality and profession (sales), values feelings.

He thinks logic is going to win the day because that's how logic is supposed to work. But, as soon as Lyn begins to feel that he's clobbering her with facts, she shuts down. *"What's the use? He's not interested in what I have to say"* is her mantra. Then Danny becomes frustrated when he sees her give up. He wants her to fight for her ideas. He's a competitor and that's what competitors do!

They've created dance steps for arguing. He lectures. She shuts down. He pushes harder. She digs in her heels (very expensive ones). Then – silence. He's frustrated and she plots to get what she wants without his help.

I asked Danny if, in an argument, he notices when Lyn is becoming passive. He said he does. *"Then, why keep hammering her with the logic?"* His response was so simple: *"I want her to see it my way."* The frustrating thing for him is that at no time has she said, *"You're right – I wasn't thinking straight."*

So why does he persist? Embarrassed, he admitted, *"It's fun – frustrating, but fun!"*

Lyn has just one goal when arguing with Danny – *"To get what I want. I'll plead and then when I get frustrated, I'll just ask, 'what do I have to do to get X?'"*

When I asked her if she asks in a tone of voice dripping with attitude she flashed a guilty smile. *"Do you pout; cross your arms, and make it sound like a demand if not an ultimatum?"* She looked shocked that I knew.

She tuned him out when he started to lecture. He tuned her out when she started to pout. No one likes a know-it-all and no one likes a whiner. And no one is going to put up with either.

So, what to do? Well, it's not possible to magically change personality; nor is there any reason to do so. However, choices can be made in how to communicate.

Lyn needs to understand that "because it feels good" is not a reason that's going to advance her cause. How do you respond to a reason like that? And Danny needs to understand that people don't always make decisions based on what's most logical.

He needs to help Lyn explore her feelings so as to help her understand what she's really thinking. And, she needs to help Danny explore his thoughts so as to help him understand what he's feeling.

Because what we think influences how we feel and how we feel influences what we think, Lyn needs to understand the reasoning that's generating her feelings and Danny needs to understand the feelings fueling his "logic."

Life is seldom lived at the extremes – it's lived in the messiness of the middle – and the middle is made up of both thoughts and feelings.

When I told all this to Danny and Lyn they each said, *"What's the point? We know how we're going to react."*

Like Danny and Lyn, do you feel frustrated that your arguments are all Groundhog's Day – a droning repetition of clichés that ultimately don't get you what you need and want?

Here's the thing – you won't know what the other person is going to say if you talk with them in a way that is different from the old dance steps. New ways of dealing with conflict will bring about new conversations.

Sanity Saver Questions ~

- Are you satisfied with the way you and your partner deal with conflict?

- What would you like to see each of you do differently?

- What does a "good fight" look like to you?

Remember:

You protect and keep each other sane when you give up the need to win, give up shutting down and when you resolve to help your partner explain what he or she is feeling, thinking and needing – and when you work to understand what you're feeling, thinking and needing.

TIP 10

You Can't Say 'Because' Too Many Times

When having a difficult conversation with your partner (relative, friend or vendor), the most important word you can say is: because.

Why? Because often times we say something without exactly explaining what we mean. Then the other person will ask, *"Why do you say that?"* Then we usually give them a "because" reason.

In Lyn's case, she would simply say, "because" without giving Danny any reason. "Because why" is what Danny was looking for.

Lyn, though, stubbornly believed that she shouldn't have to give an explanation. The truth is we all want to know the "because" for why the other person thinks, believes and acts the way they do. Giving people the "because" part of why you think something helps to give them a fuller sense of what you mean.

When having a difficult conversation with your partner it's helpful if you let your partner know "why" you think and feel the way you do because you'll give them a clearer sense of what you need from them.

Eventually, begrudgingly, Lyn admitted that she saw how she wasn't being fair to Danny "because" she didn't help him understand why she felt the way she did.

Remember:

You have a responsibility to help make it easier for your partner to understand what you need – because if you do that you'll increase your chances of getting heard and understood which will go a long way to helping you and your partner stay sane!

TIP 11

Get Out Of The "Yes, But" Cycle

Perhaps the most common "dance" that couples engage in is known as the "yes, but" dance.

This is where you seem to agree with what your partner is saying **(yes)** **AND** you're also simultaneously disagreeing as you point out why their suggestion is utterly worthless **(but)**.

For instance, consider this conversation snippet:

Groom: *"Yes, I agree that a live band would be fun, but it would put us over budget."*
Bride: *"Yes, I know our budget is tight, but we're only going to do this once."*
Groom: *"Yes, I know we're only going to do this once, but I don't want us to go over budget."*
Bride: *"Yes, I don't want to either, but a live band will make the party perfect!"*

Stop!

This couple is so polite and agreeable that their conversation is utterly useless. The two of them are going round and round and not actually tackling the issue of the band.

You have to take each other's hand and step outside the circle so as to get a different perspective on the challenge. A sure way in which you can do this is by asking questions:

- Is the budget "the" budget or is there a way to increase it?
- As you review your budget, can you make adjustments with other items so as to pay for the band?
- What is it that a band will give you that a DJ cannot?
- Have you actually looked into the cost of bands?
- Can you find a new band that's starting out and so not as pricey as one with an established rep?
- Did one of your parents offer to pay for an item that doesn't interest you much? If so, could you make the band a counter-offer?

Remember: the surest way to break the "yes, but" cycle is for you together to resolve, *"let's make this work!"*

Talk!

true story

I ran into Anna a little more than a year after her wedding. She was strolling her six-month old daughter. Sadly, she told me that she and her husband Jeff were divorcing. Things had been rocky from the start, as Jeff didn't like to talk about anything important. And when they did have that rare talk, he'd end up screaming and storming off. Anna had gotten pregnant thinking that a baby would make things "right" with her and Jeff.

I was stunned that she thought having a baby would bring them closer since a baby doesn't have that kind of power. And besides, it wasn't until the baby was born that Jeff told her he didn't want children!

If you and your partner have established your relationship in the habits of solid conversation, then that will go a long way in helping you navigate the demands of wedding planning.

If, though, you've gotten into habits of not talking face-to-face, without distractions, then you really are going to experience stress.

Sometimes, a couple argues about decisions they have to make, other times about things said and done that one of them is offended by. Over time, arguing takes on a life of its own and all the couple really does is talk at each other.

How you communicate directly affects your sanity – individually and as a couple. If you're caught up in an endless cycle of arguing, then the only way to break the cycle is to talk about how you talk to each other.

The cycle of arguing will only be broken if you take each other's hand, step out of the vicious circle, and take a look at why you're repeating the same conversation over and over and over, no matter what the issue.

Sanity Saver Questions ~

- Is there a conversation you know you should have and are afraid to have?

- What are you afraid will happen if you talk about the issue?

- What would you like to see happen differently?

Most people think the other person is to blame for the problem. Drop the blame game. As the cliché goes, it takes two to tango.

If you want to see you and your partner talk in a different way to each other, ask for your partner's help. At a time when you're not sniping at each other, tell your partner that you want to discuss how the two of you handle tough topics.

Try something like this:

Whenever we talk about finances, it seems we end up arguing. I get frustrated when you say 'no' to something I suggest and then you end the conversation. Sure, I'd want you to say 'yes' and as much as I hate to admit it, I know that 'yes' can't always be the answer. It's when you shut down, end the conversation and refuse to talk about the issue that I feel disrespected and feel that you're not treating me like a partner. I don't know what's going on inside that head of yours. I want to discuss money in a way where we don't end up mad at each other. Let's figure out something new here.

As a couple, **you're going to break old dance steps that don't work for you when you say out loud – this isn't working, so let's do something different.**

I know this does not come naturally. It takes practice. Your attitude will determine everything.

Lose the anger.
Put aside the judgment.
Accept that a tough conversation is a messy give-n-take.
That's what dialogue is all about.

Remember:

If you're afraid of what your partner's reaction might be, then I urge you to think about why you're marrying someone you're afraid of.

TIP 13

Seriously – TALK!

true story

It was six weeks before their wedding and Chad and Lisa still had not hired an officiant. Towards the end of our meeting, the conversation turned to Chad's upcoming Vegas bachelor party weekend.

After Lisa humorously warned him that nothing better happen, he reassured her with these immortal words: *"Don't worry. Nothing's going to happen even if she goes into the bedroom with me."* She? Bedroom? I'm stunned. Lisa slapped him in the arm.

Seems Chad's boys told him that they're going to get him a stripper. He didn't want a stripper, but how could he tell them that? He didn't want to ruin their fun and besides, it's tradition!

That Lisa found out about Chad's plans while at a meeting to discuss the ceremony, speaks volumes about the quality of their conversations. That he wasn't able to tell his buddies what he did and did not want, speaks volumes about his ability to assert himself.

Without being able to express what it is you're thinking, feeling, wanting and needing, it's going to be hard to offer an "I Do" that is authentic, confident and that expresses your willingness to DO all that is implied in that "I Do."

If you can't be honest with your partner before your wedding day, there's no reason to believe that you'll be able to be honest the day after your wedding day.

The German philosopher Nietzche claimed that **in its essence marriage is one long, grand conversation.**

If marriage is a conversation, do you and your partner enjoy talking with each other?

When I meet with couples as they create their wedding ceremony, I give them the following list of questions. Perhaps a few of these will spark a new conversation between you and your partner.

1. When people speak of your wedding, what three words do you want them to say? What three words do you not want them to say?

2. Is your wedding day a beginning or a touch point in your life together?

3. What was the most moving, most joyful wedding you've attended? What do you want to be the most joyful moment of your wedding day?

4. Who are your role models for marriage? Why? How realistic a model are they?

5. Is your partner your life OR does your partner give you life?

6. What makes your partner worthy of your love? What makes you worthy of your partner's love?

7. What are your expectations of each other? Do your expectations make each of you the best you are capable of being?

8. What is your biggest fear for your life together?

9. What is your definition of success? As an individual? As a couple?

10. On you 25th wedding anniversary, what would you like to look back upon?

Remember:

You protect and keep each other safe when you talk with each other.
Really talk – openly, trustingly, from the silly to the serious.
You can't plan your wedding without talking.

TIP 14

Listen With Your Eye

true story

I asked Charlene and Terry if they'd like me to conclude the ceremony with a blessing. They both said that they were not religious, though they believed in God. Terry added that Charlene believed more than he did.

Charlene asked Terry what he wanted. He said he didn't care and then asked her what she wanted. She said it *"might be nice to have a blessing."* Terry simultaneously agreed and disagreed when he said, *"Yeah, it doesn't bother me either way, so, yeah, we don't need to have one."* Clearly Charlene looked disappointed as she asked him, "Wouldn't it be nice if we had some mention of God?" Not only did Terry not hear what she was saying, he didn't "hear" the look on her face and so he answered, *"No, it doesn't matter to me, but I don't see the point."*

Charlene now upped the ante – *"Well, I always imagined having a blessing at the wedding."* Steadfastly clueless, Terry tried to end the discussion with, *"Okay, so we'll talk about it."* Charlene's eyes lowered and she tilted her head, clearly signaling that she was unhappy.

At this point, I jumped in, assuring Terry that he was getting a blessing. I turned to Charlene: *"He's getting a blessing, right?"* She laughed and thanked me. Poor Terry still seemed clueless as to how he ended up with a blessing.

I'm not entirely sure why Terry didn't realize Charlene was telling him that she'd really like a blessing

However, had he looked at her and really seen the expression of her face, he would have picked up that this was something important to her. Instead, he simply brushed aside the words because he didn't want to deal with them.

It's easy to stop paying attention without even being aware, not because you've stopped loving your partner, but rather, because you're so busy or you're weary from talking about a particular aspect of the wedding. And because you love each other it's easy to think, "we'll he knows I love him," or "she knows that I support her."

"Knowing" isn't enough. We need to be reassured, especially in times of stress.

Simply looking at your partner and not being distracted with multi-tasking is a great act of reassurance.

Simply saying to your partner, *"I know this is important to you and I'm not in a place to give it my real attention. Can we come back to this?"* is a great act of reassurance.

The most reassuring of reassurances are conveyed in mindful little ways.

Sanity Saver Questions ~

- When listening to your partner, how well are you able to "read" their non-verbal signals?

- When you don't want to listen to what your partner has to say, how do you let them know?

- Which do you pay more attention to – words or body language?

Remember:

Important conversations involve both the eye and the ear.

TIP 15

Listen With Your Heart

true story

After a menu tasting, Donna called me as she was feeling utterly dumbfounded. She needed a reality check. Donna and her fiancé, Tony, selected asparagus as their main course vegetable. Donna's mother, who had insisted on going to the tasting, suddenly snapped, *"No one likes asparagus; what are you thinking?"* Tony pointed out that many people like asparagus. Donna's mother would not hear of it. Tony and Donna decided on peas. The mother was happy.

Bizarre? Well, yeah! And sometimes it all comes down to asparagus.

Donna decided to have a heart-to-heart with her mother and soon learned that her mother was feeling left out of the planning. She herself never had a wedding reception. She wasn't necessarily a "Mom-zilla." She just wanted to feel needed – and her daughter had never asked for her help in any aspect of the planning. The only way this mother knew how to make herself needed was to pick on the poor asparagus!

And why hadn't Donna asked her mother for advice and help? While she loved her mother she always struggled with her mother's enthusiastic ways that slipped into being overbearing. She was afraid that if she asked for help, her mother would overwhelm her.
After the asparagus incident Donna made it a point to get her mother's input on more of the non-essential decisions. Her mother was happy and so was Donna.

Because wedding planning is an emotional roller coaster, a lot of the listening that goes on is not just about details. It's about the feelings accompanying all those detail oriented tasks.

Whether listening to your mother or to your partner it's important to listen to what's not being said, to what's fueling the (weird) words that the person is saying to you.

You need to reassure your partner that you take seriously what they're feeling (even if you think that what triggered those feelings is silly).

Sanity Saver Questions ~

- How well can you intuit when something is troubling your partner?

- What is your "dance step" for when you're partner seems unwilling to open up?

- How comfortable are you asking, "hey, what's going on?"

Remember:

Important conversations demand that you dig deep beneath the obvious to what might be the real cause of the confusion, discomfort or annoyance.

It means helping the other person figure out what they themselves might not even be consciously aware of.

TIP 16

Laugh!

true story

I was going to officiate a wedding at the Terrranea Resort in Rancho Palos Verdes, CA. It's an expansive, gracious venue about forty minutes from LAX. Since I'd arrived early for the wedding, I found a table on the patio outside the lobby where I could check-up on email and messages.

A few chairs away from me sat a couple (early thirties) playing cards. Coronas were on the table and I spotted wedding rings on each of them. They were laughing and being silly, looking like a couple of kids having fun on an Autumn afternoon.

At one point, the guy's phone rang. He glanced at it but then ignored it, took a swig of beer and went back to the cards. The woman said something, swatted him on the arm and he cracked up.

What most struck me was just how relaxed they looked – how affectionately "at one" they were in their relaxation. They were lost in their own world and seemed beyond delighted to be there.

What about you and your partner – can you be silly with each other? Even while planning your wedding?

British designer Paul Smith (a favorite of mine) attributes much of his success to this: *"Every day of my life I witness something that makes me burst out laughing."*

Wow! Now that's a skill.

What about you? Are you laughing?

Are you feeling happy? If not, what's going on? What's draining you and what can you and your partner actively do to restore your ability to laugh.

Remember:

Getting married is a serious undertaking. Throwing a wedding is a serious undertaking. And that's why you have got to laugh!

If you're doing more stressing and more crying than laughing, then something is out of alignment.

TIP 17

See-saw Your Way Out Of Being Stuck

true story

Amy and Peggy had firmly resolved to stay within budget, but Amy wanted an open bar and Peggy wanted to feed the guests a meal. They couldn't do both. They were disheartened and tough on each other.

Amy thought an open bar was a sign of hospitality to family and friends. Peggy thought a meal was a sign of generosity. Over several conversations what they realized is that they wanted two key things. First, they both wanted their guests to feel welcomed and appreciated. Second, they both wanted to create a fun time.

What they eventually came up with satisfied both requirements. They opted for a cocktail party reception – great drinks, fab finger food (lots of it), a cake to die-for and a hot DJ. All within budget. They got what they both wanted – a fun party that treated their guests to the best of what they could afford. All of which at the beginning had not seemed possible.

For Amy and Peggy the trick was to see the issues, the speed bumps, from each other's perspective and then tinker with ideas that turned their original demands upside-down and so give each of them a new perspective.

When challenges arise in your planning, more times than not, all you really have to do is look at the problem from a new and unfamiliar angle.

Yes, these new and unfamiliar angles are not always easy to come by, especially because it's so easy to focus on what seems impossible. Instead, focus on the heart of what you want and don't fixate on the specifics that often present themselves as insurmountable challenges.

As soon as Peggy and Amy stopped focusing on meal vs. open bar, they were able to strategize on how to get what they really wanted – a party where their guests felt welcomed and cared for.

Sanity Saver Questions ~

- What is a planning issue that you and your partner are "stuck" on?

- What are the reasons you haven't been able to find a solution?

- What is it that you really want?

- Is there a way to get what you want even if the solution looks different from what you'd originally envisioned?

Remember:

Whatever the challenge, it is temporary. From all my years of celebrating weddings, I know that there is no wedding challenge that cannot be resolved.

Tip 18

Don't Get Trapped By Your 'Family Motto'

true story

When not officiating weddings, I'm a corporate communications coach and trainer (thebusinessofconfidence.com). In addition, I teach business and cross-cultural communication courses at UCLA Extension. This email excerpt is from Rose, a student, explaining why she missed the last class. All of this does have something to do with wedding planning – trust me!

"I'm so sorry that I missed last night's last class. I was in the car on the way there and ended up having a tough conversation with my parents about wedding planning - the source of many of our family's conversations these days.

We ended up talking on the phone for two hours and it was such an important conversation for us to have that I made the tough call to continue on and miss class.

The most important thing I've gained from the course is the idea of the "family motto." My family and my fiance's family have completely different family mottos and it's been clouding the way that everyone communicates with each other.

My family's motto is 'wear your heart on your sleeve' and his is 'keep your cards close to your chest.' Our parents have had so many misunderstandings and disagreements and it's all a result of them not understanding where the other ones are coming from.

My parents are transparent and want everyone to share their feelings during our meetings and discussions and his parents just don't operate that way. This has resulted in my fiance and I putting ourselves in the middle, which has turned into a giant game of telephone, which we ended last night.

After asking our parents to talk directly to each other, we had conversations with each set of parents and it became clear that our mottos are in conflict.

And it was because of what I learned in your class that I was able to take control of the conversation and get everyone to realize we're all operating towards the same goal but we're getting there different ways."

So what is this "family motto" thing that Rose referred to? Well, let me tell you another –

true story

When Paulann and Paul hired me they'd not yet chosen a venue. He had a large family and wanted a place where they could invite everyone "plus one." She had a small immediate and extended family and didn't care (so she claimed) where they got married.

As the weeks passed, they still hadn't found the right place and were bickering to a degree that surprised each of them. She nixed every venue he liked and he began to wonder if she even wanted to get married.

When we got together it was clear that they were working from different visions of their day, guided by what I call family mottos.

Our family's beliefs and rituals are like the air we breathe. Every family lives life guided by a motto, a mantra. Sometimes it is spoken aloud; other times it is implicitly understood. But no matter, this motto guides a family as it navigates through life.

When I was growing up, my family's motto was, "trust no one." My father was a cop. His job demanded that he be leery of all. And as is often the case, his work flowed into his home. I breathed in that mantra without thought or doubt. Later in life I had to work hard to overcome its limitations and trust people.

When growing up, Paul's home was where all the neighborhood kids wanted to hang out. His mother loved to cook. His family made a good fuss over holidays and birthdays. "The more the merrier" was their motto.

Paulann's family was close-knit and very private. Few of her friends were ever invited for dinner. Holidays and birthdays were celebrated in a low-key way. By nine o'clock the dishes were done and everyone was heading to bed. "Proper" was the guiding word in her family life.

Paul saw their wedding as the celebration of all celebrations. Paulann didn't want to share her day with so many people.

What to do?

Talk.

They had to talk openly and trustingly. They had to have some hard conversations, revealing feelings that surprised each of them.

Once they were able to see things from each other's perspective, they were able to go about making honest decisions that honored them both. They were able to set about creating a new family motto – one that was their very own.

Sanity Saver Questions ~

- How were you taught to see life? What is your family's motto regarding life?

- How was your partner taught to see life? What is your partner's family's motto?

- How do those assumptions about life influence you in your life together? As you plan your wedding?

Remember:

Without understanding your family's and your partner's family's assumptions about how life is lived, you will be setting yourself up in subtle ways for the stress of misunderstanding.

If your family's mantra limits you and your partner, then toss it to the side. Choose a new mantra that reflects who you are and who you want to be!

TIP 19

Check Your Perceptions

true story

At our final meeting, I double-checked with Bella that she still had six bridesmaids. She told me that she now only had five. Seems one of her bridesmaids didn't make the bridal shower and didn't tell her beforehand. And this wasn't the first time she flaked on a wedding related date. Bella explained to her friend that since she didn't have her back, there was no point in having her remain in the wedding party.

I was surprised to learn that Bella never asked her friend why she'd been consistently flaking on her bridesmaid's duties. She said she didn't have time for drama or for seeking out excuses. Bella's actually not a Bridezilla and she believed her decision was the honest thing to do. But was it the only thing she could have done?

Often times, what is most obvious is not most true. While the bridesmaid didn't have Bella's back, Bella dismissed her without ever finding out what was going on – was she a thoughtless flake or was there another explanation?

Yes, it's true that people can say and do some really strange and downright irritating things to an engaged couple. Perhaps you've noticed?!

However, if a friend or family member is acting in ways that confuse or frustrate you, and the relationship is important to you, then take the time to do something known as: Perception Checking.

Bella presumed that her bridesmaid flaked because she didn't care.

Maybe.

BUT

Bella doesn't know the real reason because she never checked what was going on. She didn't check her perceptions.

Perception Checking is done in four steps:

1. Ask your friend for some time to talk in person if possible. If not, then by phone (or Skype). Don't try this via email or text.

2. Describe for them the pattern of behavior that's confusing you – no judgments or interpretations – just the facts. For instance, they weren't able to go with you when you picked out your dress / tux, they haven't helped with the shower, etc.

3. Offer TWO possible interpretations for why this pattern is happening, i.e. *"I don't know if work has been busy for you and you haven't been able to get away or if I've done something to hurt you."*

4. Then ask them to clarify: I'm confused and I want to make sure that you do have my back, so what's going on?

If they say "nothing," then repeat the steps, stating the pattern, offering other possible interpretations, that you need their support and that if they're not able to give it that's okay. You just want clarity.

These four steps will increase the chances that your friend or relative (or partner) will not become defensive and instead will engage you in open conversation.

If they do resist, become defensive or get "weird," then you can decide to disinvite them to you wedding. This is not punishment; rather it's an honest act of honoring you and your partner and your mutual sanity.

Remember:

Everyone does what they do for a reason – and that reason may not always be evident to you. If the relationship is important and you need clarity about what's going on – don't presume. Ask!

TIP 20

Vaccinate Yourself

true story

Matthew's aunt Debbie arrived four hours early to the hotel. Wandering around, she bumped into, Doris, the event planner, who was stressing out because an afternoon wedding was in full swing in the ballroom where Matthew and Eddie's wedding ceremony was going to take place. Doris would have just one hour for the turn-around.

Doris suggested that Matthew's aunt enjoy a lite lunch in the café. No, she didn't want to spoil her appetite. Perhaps tea in the lounge? No, too noisy. Visit with Matthew's and Eddie's mothers who were having their make-up done? No, didn't want to intrude. A nice walk around the beach neighborhood? Bad hip. Doris was losing patience with each increasingly annoyed rejection. Lucky for Doris, poor Matthew and a couple of his attendants walked by and she handed aunt-pain-in-the-butt off to them!

Doris was attentive and respectful to this woman. She acted like a pro. But Aunt Debbie was also a pro. Turns out, she'd had a long history of being demanding at family functions and so, no one was surprised that she was making a fuss with Doris. *"Oh, that's just how Aunt Debbie is!"*

Here's the thing, if you have a Debbie (or two) in your family, don't expect them to change just because you're getting married. People are consistent. Family rituals and dynamics hold strong.

So what can you do?

5 tips for 'vaccinating' yourself against annoying relatives – before they get to your wedding

1. Knowing what you know about your own "Aunt Debbie" do you want that person(s) at your wedding? If you don't, then why are you inviting them? Family politics? Fair enough. Because your mother or father insists that they come? Fine. Just make sure you get them to agree to take care of this demanding relative.

2. If political fallout will be minimal and/or containable, then consider not inviting the person(s). You simply explain that you're keeping the wedding small.

3. How is the person annoying? If they are not "dangerous," in that they don't pose a threat to the overall well-being of the day, then perhaps there's a way you can show them a little of the attention they crave. More times than not, a difficult person is simply seeking attention. You could give them a task, i.e. oversee the guest book; ask them to do something, i.e. a reading.

4. If they are "dangerous," in that their behavior is unpredictable, then the week before your wedding you need to have a talk and let them know what you need from them, i.e. a promised agreement that they will be on "best behavior." Ask someone to keep an eye on the person the day of the wedding. If you have an event planner or on-site coordinator, let them be aware of the situation.

If you've decided to invite the person(s) then don't complain about them! You knew what you were getting when you invited them. AND, don't worry about them – you've arranged for them to be taken care of. You've handled it and now others will handle it for you, if need be.

Remember:

It is your day and if people can't share your joy then that's their decision and not your problem – although you are responsible for vaccinating yourself against any and all potential "problems."

TIP 21

Talk With Your Parents

true story

Jeannie and Nelson were getting married at a four-star country club. Jeannie's parents had agreed to pay for the reception. Two weeks before the wedding, her dad called to inform them that he rechecked his finances and was making changes to the menu. Without consulting with Jeannie and Nelson, he arbitrarily changed the surf-n-turf to chopped sirloin, cancelled the wedding cake and substituted it with just ice cream.

Jeannie was devastated but too embarrassed to feel angry with her father. Nelson, on the other hand, was livid as this was not the first time her dad had pulled an inexplicably nasty stunt on them. So, he decided to call the old man's bluff.

Without conferring with Jeannie, Nelson informed his soon-to-be father-in-law that he and Jeannie were postponing the wedding until such times as they could afford their original plans. Now it was the father's turn to feel embarrassed.

When Jeannie found out what Nelson had done, she took all of her anger out on him. A day later, Jeannie's dad suddenly "found" money and the menu was restored. By now, though, Jeannie and Nelson weren't talking to each other!

Often times, the hardest conversations center on parents – yours and / or your partner's.

How comfortable are you talking honestly about your feelings towards your parents?

Does your partner even know how you feel about their folks?

Sanity Saver Questions ~

- How do you handle difficult conversations with your parents? Revert back to childhood? Become passive-aggressive? Argue heatedly?

- Have you been able to honestly talk to your parents about what you want and don't want for your wedding?

- Have you asked your parents for specific help in any areas?

- What do you think are your parents' obligations to your wedding in terms of planning and / or helping to pay?

- What are you willing and / or prepared to do if your parents don't like your ideas?

- Is your wedding family-focused or friend-focused?

- How can you show your family thanks throughout the planning process?

Remember:

You and your partner will keep each other sane by being united in your vision and being willing to discuss that vision with your parents – together and individually.

TIP 22

Be Honest With Your Parents

true story

Ellie's father had refused to give his blessing to her and her fiancé Sean. For five years he held back. Finally and somewhat begrudgingly he gave his approval. He reached this place because both Ellie and Sean, were patient and, in my opinion, generous in their consideration of his feelings.

Ellie shared with me a letter she had written her dad. It was over six pages, single-spaced and I, who seldom cry, was misty-eyed by the end.

As a bride or groom, I know that you have your own story with your parents. If one or both of your parents are withholding support and blessing, you might appreciate what Ellie wrote her dad. This is an edited version of her letter.

Dear Dad,

Sean is my best friend. He works 30-hour shifts with the pager going off constantly, trauma patients coming in, the doctors asking for help, the nurses calling for orders, the patients and families wanting someone to talk to – it's chaotic. And after all that he goes home exhausted and he still finds it in himself to call me, talk to me like I'm a human being, ask me how my day was. He listens to me complain about school and how I'm exhausted and he helps me through it. He never gets angry at me, he never gets impatient, never tells me that my problems are insignificant compared to his.

Since I've met him he has never once raised his voice at me, never disrespected me, never made me feel inferior and even in the most stressful times in his own life he's never taken his emotions out on me. He understands me, appreciates me, takes care of me and always knows exactly what I want. He makes me smile when I need to, lets me whine when I want to and is always there for me through everything.

The only thing that makes this picture incomplete is the fact that you decided long ago that you dislike him. You think he's unreliable but what you haven't seen is how he always keeps his word and follows through with the things he says. You think that he can't stay faithful but I've never met a more faithful person to his friends, his family, his colleagues and to me.

I know you liked Brandon but that wasn't a relationship I could have stayed in. When he got grumpy he was unpleasant, after 10 hours at work he would be snappy, if he was unhappy about one thing he was unhappy about everything, including me. I always doubted myself, always figured I was doing something wrong, I always wanted to know what I could fix or do better. I thought that the cost of knowing what he was thinking was having to deal with his raw emotions.

Little did I know that there could be someone who would tell me everything they were feeling but at the same time realize that I wasn't the source of his negative emotions, I was the cure for them and there was no need to take his anger out on me.

I know the type of person that you are trying to protect me from; but time and time again Sean has shown me that he is not that type of person. I don't want to lose my family over this. I'd like to be able to have a calm conversation with you about this without any yelling or arguing.

Love,
Ellie

A moving letter, yes?

If you've been to a lot of weddings, chances are you've heard the classic excerpt from St. Paul's letter to the Corinthians, "Love is patient, love is kind." It's a powerful reading, but because it has been heard so many times at weddings, it's lost its force.

Here's a modern translation of Paul's letter. What strikes me is how similar Paul's words on love are to the words Ellie uses to describe the love she shares with Sean.

Love never gives up.

Love cares more for others than for self.

Love doesn't want what it doesn't have.

Love doesn't strut,

Doesn't force itself on others,

Isn't always "me first,"

Doesn't fly off the handle,

Doesn't keep score of the sins of others,

Doesn't revel when others grovel,

Takes pleasure in the flowering of truth,

Puts up with anything,

Always looks for the best,

Never looks back,

But keeps going to the end.

Love never dies: trust steadily, hope unswervingly, love extravagantly.

And the best of the three is love.

Remember:

A wedding celebrates something extraordinary – your love for each other – and your love is extraordinary.

Tip 23

Share This Letter With Your Parents If They're Divorced

Dear Divorced Parents,

I love weddings for many reasons, chief among them being that I love stories. As an officiant I hear a lot of stories. Stories that make me laugh and that inspire me or simply gobsmack me with their whack-a-do-ness! And then there are the heart-aching stories, many of which involve parents who happen to be divorced.

Not all "my parents are divorced" stories are tragic. In fact, I've met divorced parents who have somehow managed to remain friends – and who genuinely like the new spouses.

But then there are the other stories – stories of unhealed hurt and bitterness that propel people into saying and doing things that are astounding.

Bradley's Catholic parents divorced when he was seven years old. His mother, who attends daily Mass, told him that if he invited his father's wife (of ten years) she would not be able to attend the wedding.

Janet's mother told her that if she asked her father to escort her down the aisle, she wouldn't attend the wedding because the sight of him smiling would make her sick.

Alice asked her mom and step-dad (who had raised her) to walk her down the aisle. But her father was paying for the reception and he wanted to walk her down the aisle even though he had disappeared from her life when she was ten and only re-emerged three years ago. And, yes, he threatened to not pay for the reception if her mom and step-dad walked her down the aisle.

Caryl's parents divorced when she was ten years old. Her father remarried a year later. Caryl developed a warm relationship with her step-mom. Eventually, her father divorced her step-mom, but Caryl remained friends with her.

Caryl's mother is now engaged and her father is again engaged – to a woman eight years older than Caryl. Caryl's step-mom is remarried. All six people will be present at the wedding!

Caryl's father hasn't talked to her mother in years. Caryl's mother and first step-mom can't stomach her father's fiancée and don't want her in any family portraits. And the fiancée? Well, she's demanding a corsage identical to the one Caryl's mom is wearing.

Are you confused? Do you hear just how outrageous all of this is?!

When Caryl began to explain the "flow-chart" to me, she was laughing at the absurdity of it all. By the end of our conversation, she was crying. And Tony, her fiancé, whose own parents have been happily married for thirty-five years, looked on concerned and bewildered.

The pressures of dealing with the pain of seeing so much hatred among people she loves, has taken its toll on Caryl. She's weary from the demands that each of these people is making on her.

As both an officiant and a communications coach, I offered her some tips on how to assert herself and set boundaries. But what she needs is more than "tips."

What she needs is KINDNESS.

She needs for each of these people to be kind to her and to her fiancé. She needs them, at the very least, to be civil and sensible with each other.

And so, as you grapple with your own pain, which does need to be respected, I plead with you to not let your pain cause you to forget about your daughter or son, who is trying to be a peacemaker, who is trying to respect her or his relationship with your ex-spouse, who does not want to add to your hurt, yet who cannot bear the burden of your pain.

I'm not demeaning or dismissing your raw feelings. Now, though, you have the opportunity and the responsibility to offer your child all the kindness they deserve.

I don't know the story of your divorce – and maybe your daughter or son doesn't even know the full story. But as an officiant, I can tell you that I am saddened from meeting brides and grooms whose hearts are torn by the flame-tossing insensitivity of their divorced parents. I know it's not your intention to hurt your child – but you are. In more ways than you know.

It's been said that the "truth hurts," so here is the truth – you simply don't have the right to douse your child and their partner with your anger and bitterness. Surely, this is not the wedding gift you want to give them?

STOP the demands. STOP the ultimatums. STOP the drama.

You do have the power to stop the madness.

Your daughter or son deserves the best of who you are on their wedding celebration. How can you even think of offering them anything less? Get the support you need – and deserve. Ask your son or daughter to recognize your pain. Ask without emotionally blackmailing them. And then ask them what they need from you.

Even though I don't know you, I am going to ask you, on behalf of your son or daughter, to do what may be the bravest thing you've ever done:

Bless them through your hurt and pain – and don't let that hurt and pain cause you to hurt them on their day of hope and renewal.

TIP 24

Strategize Difficult Conversations

I originally had posted on The Huffington Post the Tip 23 open letter to the divorced parents of a bride or groom.

A few months after it was published I received an email from Roger, a divorced father whose daughter, Susan, was getting married later in the year. Roger wrote that my "letter" helped him realize that more than anything he wants to be emotionally present for his daughter and future son-in-law.

Roger and his wife divorced when Susan was little. His ex-wife eventually married Jack who has been a huge part of Susan's life as her step-dad. While Roger is not a buddy with his ex-wife and Jack they have always respected one another. And all three are contributing to the cost of the wedding.

Yes, there is a 'but'!

Susan has asked Roger to escort her down the aisle and she and her fiancé, Brad, have asked Jack to officiate the ceremony (he'll be getting ordained online). Roger feels confused and slighted as it appears that Jack is being given a larger and more important role in the wedding celebration. In addition, Roger's family is Jewish and Jack is not. What will people say if there's no rabbi? To his credit, Roger doesn't like feeling petty. On the other hand, he doesn't like feeling confused. He asked me what he should do.

I only know what Roger told me and so, of course, there are several sides to this story. Whatever the "real" and full story might be, Roger is not the first parent to feel slighted by the decisions of a bride and groom – and you don't have to be divorced to feel confused!

Here are some pointers I offered Roger –

Start from the belief that no slight is intended.

Roger said that he had a good relationship with Susan, as did her step-dad Jack, so we can legitimately presume that Susan and Brad are seeking to do their best. The great traditional honor is for a father to escort his daughter down the aisle. Because Susan's fiancé is not Jewish and because Susan's step-dad is not Jewish and because Susan and her fiancé have decided to have a non-denominational ceremony, it makes sense why they would ask her step-dad. He is an ideal officiant (theoretically) in that he appeals to both sides.

It doesn't matter what people think. I know – simple for me to say!

I gently reminded Roger that his mother is deceased and so it doesn't matter if she would have been disappointed that her only granddaughter is not being married by a rabbi. The dear woman no longer has to worry about such things! I urged him not to worry about what people will say because if anyone objects to Susan not being married by a rabbi, then, they should stay home and binge watch their fav TV series. A wedding is a day for joy and not judgment.

Trust your relationship with Susan and ask her to help you sort out your feelings by explaining her decision.

I reminded Roger that he is not asking Susan to get his permission for anything; rather, he's simply asking her to help him make sense of a new type of celebration because he wants to be fully present for her and Brad.

I went on to suggest that, if possible, Roger, his ex-wife and Jack, together with the couple, explore how to broaden the scope of the ceremony so it's not focused on Jack and is more inclusive of both families – after all, Brad has parents!

- Both mothers could do a reading (they alternate stanzas).
- All three dads could give the blessing at ceremony's end.
- Jack could make clear in his opening remarks that he speaks on behalf of all the parents.

Roger liked what I had to say, but let's face it – all of this is tricky because people see a wedding from different perspectives. When it comes to communicating with family, we rely on our default settings, especially when buttons get pressed.

So the question Roger needs to ask is, *"What can I do differently, so as to get heard and understood, so as to hear and understand?"*

Roger assured me that he was going to talk with his daughter because even though it would be a hard conversation to have, more than anything, he did not want to end up causing her pain. And besides, he wanted to enjoy every minute of her wedding. But in order to do that, he had to clear up his confusion.

Again, the ultimate question, whose answer will guide all your decisions is this: "Who do you want to be – for the couple – during one of the seminal times in their life together?"

PS: I didn't have the opportunity to speak with Susan and Brad. If I had, though, this is what I would have suggested to them:

As a bride, as a groom, as a couple, it's easy to become so focused on what you want, that you can presume much, too much, of those you love.

To reduce miscommunication, practice these 5 strategies:

- No surprises – keep all VIPs in the loop throughout the planning.

- Be honest in talking with parental units – no guilt-tripping (no matter how tempting or potentially rewarding).

- Don't assume responsibility for your parents' feelings. This isn't about "making" them happy. However, don't trample their feelings.

- "Because" – that simple word goes a long way to bringing about understanding. People appreciate understanding the "why" behind a decision.

- Keep channels open – "this is what I need from you" can probably never be said too many times!

Remember:

You can disagree and still love!

TIP 25

Learn From The Reality Of A Reality Show Wedding

true story

I had the honor of officiating the wedding of Rob Mariano and Amber Brkich, reality show sweethearts who met while competing on *Survivor*. In true reality show fashion, their wedding preparations and celebration became a special on CBS-TV. Celebrity event planner Colin Cowie created the detailed graciousness of their wedding at The Atlantis Resort in the Bahamas. And, yes, by any standard this was the stuff of fairy tale weddings.

While the budget was beyond that of the average wedding, the producers and Colin very much wanted Rob & Amber's wedding to be a "wedding" and not a reality TV spectacle.

When I returned home, family and friends pounded me with questions about the "perfect fairy tale wedding." Yet, oddly, at no point did I think of it as the perfect wedding. I've always thought that Colin and the producers and vendors, along with family and friends, gifted Rob and Amber with a magical wedding.

Yes, as weddings go, it was perfect. Colin and the producers worked mightily and generously. Yet, there was a storm brewing and we didn't know until an hour before the start if we could hold the ceremony on the beach. It was so windy that Amber's veil got entangled in an entry arch and almost yanked her off her feet. Not seen on TV was all the stress, worry and holding of breath that is related to weddings.

The ceremony's backdrop of a magnificent sunset and windy ocean was magical. And the magic continued throughout the reception as we sat at long tables and shared food family style. Stories were told that made people roar with laughter. Through the wee hours magic was kicked up on the dance floor.

Rob and Amber, their family, friends and all the good folk who worked on their wedding created a memory of unbridled life.

They created magic – a moment in time when people can remember what is most important in life – family and friends, love and loyalty.

And that is the stuff that no TV crew can produce – the "stuff" more long lasting than perfection.

true story

I met with Barbara, a young bride who had seen Rob & Amber's wedding. The first question she asked me was, *"Do you need a lot of money to have a great wedding?"*

The simple answer is no, you don't need a lot of money.

Money doesn't buy "magic" or guarantee a great party. I've been to weddings with six-figure budgets and I was bored out of my mind. I've been to very economical weddings and I was bored out of mind.

What do you need to have a great celebration?

People who love you.

Rob's and Amber's families and friends reveled in the love they brought – in all the good will and wackiness that came with them. That all this was going to be on TV certainly added to the fun, but it's not what gave the celebration its heart.

Sanity Saver Questions ~

- What are five things you want people to say about your wedding?

- How many of those things require more money than you have now?

- How will your wedding be diminished if you don't have the elements you can't afford?

Remember:

Magic does not happen magically. You and your partner create magic – along with those you enlist to support and help you in the planning.

The magic comes from imagining and talking. From being grateful for the life you have created and the life you are determined to continue to create.

BONUS

8 Things I Know For Sure About Weddings

I have officiated over one thousand wedding ceremonies. More times than not, couples inevitably tell me that they're worried they're going to ball their eyes out.

I laugh and encourage them not to worry because my experience has been that the brides and grooms who say they will cry often times don't while the ones who say they're not going to cry end up needing a paper bag to breathe into! I say, "cry!" – make-up can be reapplied.

But why are weddings such an emotional experience? Maybe it's because a wedding, in its essence, is a breathtaking act of generosity and courage.

After all these years, after all these weddings, here are the 8 Things I Know For Certain About Weddings, no matter the size of the guest list, no matter the faith, culture or sexual orientation of the couple.

1. Every couple has a story AND every bride and groom IS a story

We need a witness to our lives. In a marriage, you're promising to care about everything. The good things, the bad things, the terrible things, the mundane things – all of it, all of the time, every day. You're saying 'Your life will not go unnoticed because I will notice it. Your life will not go un-witnessed because I will be your witness.'

Shall We Dance?

I love listening to a couple tell me the story of how they met because in the telling I get a glimpse of who each person is. In listening to how they were surprised by love, listening to why they are grateful to their partner, I get a glimpse into the story of who they are.

I marvel at how all couples are similar AND how all are vastly different. Each has a story of how they got to the point of planning a wedding with this person out of all the billions of people in the world.

Because a wedding celebrates the co-mingling of stories I feel inspired and cheered, challenged and moved, and, yes, sometimes, just plain puzzled!

2. The planning process gives clear evidence of what the strengths and weaknesses are of the couple – as a couple

To fall in love is easy,
But it is a hard quest worth making
To find a comrade
Through whose steady presence
One becomes the person one desires to be.

Anna Louise Strong

No matter how intimate or how large the guest list, a wedding presses buttons that trigger everything from anxious insecurity to indescribable joy. And if you pay attention, all those stressors, all those reactions to those stressors, indicate who the person you're marrying is at this point in time.

The quality of how you communicate during the planning reveals the quality of your life after the honeymoon.

3. A wedding speaks to the core aspects of a couple's identity – family, culture and religion.

Explore and discover that which is within.
When we find ourselves, we are more easily found by others.

Lao Tzu

In order to say "I Do!" there needs to be an "I" and the planning of a wedding invites, challenges and demands that each person ask, "Who Am I?" in relation to their place within a family, within a culture and within (or without) a belief system. What have you incorporated from each? What have you rejected? And how has all of that gone into making the "I" who will say "I Do"?

4. A wedding calls forth memories – good, bad and glorious.

In that book which is my memory,
On the first page of the chapter that is the day when I first met you,
Appear the words, 'Here begins a new life'.

Dante

A wedding is a grateful celebration for the past. From the moment of the proposal on up to the last dance, accurately or inaccurately remembered memories trigger emotions. And all those memories influence how you react to stress, along with what you expect and ask of your partner, your family and your circle of friends.

5. A wedding challenges a couple's relationships with family and friends.

*The best part of life is when your family become your friends
and your friends become your family*

Danica Whitfield

People can forget that the wedding is not about them. People you thought you could rely upon disappear because of their own mystifying reasons. People on your "B List" generously surprise you. Parents speak and act out of love laced with protective fear in ways that can confuse, exasperate or delight. Parents want the celebration to reflect a reality that simply doesn't exist or that doesn't match the reality of who you are as a couple. Weddings challenge your capacity for surprise.

6. A wedding is an act of faith

However richly inspired by love,
Marriage is a high wire act
That is usually attempted by two nervous wrecks
Who just go for it,
Reeling with bliss and blind with the hots.
The rest is work, faith and destiny.

Unknown

Each of you only knows so much of who you are today. There are aspects of "you" that you've not yet explored and figured out – and so it is with your partner. The great act of faith is that you say, "I'm going to create a future with you. Of all the people with whom I could create a future, I choose you because you have, united with me, what I need to create a life-giving future – for me, for us." Because we can't predict the future a marriage is a glorious high wire act.

7. A wedding challenges a couple to ask what they want from and for their own life

Love is our true destiny. We do not find the meaning of life by ourselves alone – we find it in another. The meaning of our life is a secret that has to be revealed to us in love, by the one we love. Whoever loves is more alive and more real than when they did not love.

Thomas Merton

If you don't have goals and dreams and hopes, then why bother getting married? The great gift of marriage is that it gives you the safety to become who you desire to become – provided you and your partner have shared with each other and have already learned how to encourage those goals, dreams and hopes!

8. A wedding allows us to fulfill our collective, innate need to celebrate

There are only two ways to live your life: one is as though nothing is a miracle. The other is as though everything is a miracle.

Einstein

Ritual (religious or not) grounds us and helps us make sense of life. In a world seemingly gone mad, a wedding has the power to reassure us that life is good – and worthy of our best. Every wedding reminds us of the lasting truth stated by Emily Dickinson:
That Love is all there is,
Is all we know of Love.

Given these 8 certainties, is it any wonder that we cry at weddings?!

ABOUT JP REYNOLDS

Ordained a Catholic priest, JP Reynolds today works as a non-denominational wedding officiant. During the last twenty+ years, he has celebrated over 1000 weddings – non-denominational, inter-faith, cross-cultural, same-sex. He has created wedding ceremonies that honor the cultural sensitivities of couples that are as spiritually diverse as Muslim/Hindu and Buddhist/Jewish.

His wedding ceremonies have been seen on Lifetime, The Style Network, VH-1, E! Entertainment and The WE where he appeared on Bridezillas. In 2005 he officiated the wedding of Rob and Amber, reality show sweethearts from Survivor and The Amazing Race.

JP has collaborated with some of the industry's top event planners and is Brides Magazine preferred officiant for their annual Brides Live Wedding Event.

In addition to his responsibilities as a wedding officiant, JP is an executive coach and founder of The Business of Confidence (JPBOC.com). He coaches people how to present themselves with insight and confidence. His clients range from the not-for-profit sector to the Fortune 500.

JP regularly lectures on issues of business communication and relationships at UCLA Extension and blogs with HuffPo.

JP can be reached with your questions and comments at:

JP@JPRWeddings.com

JPRWeddings.com

Also From JP Reynolds

BOOKS

How To Write Your Vows:
Giving Voice To What Is Deep Within

Is an invitation to slow down and look into your heart as you prepare to offer vows to your partner. I explain the four options for composing your vows and offer basic tips on how to actually say your vows.

Bonus Chapters offer samplings of traditional vows as well as words for exchanging rings.In addition, I help you reflect on what it is you want to say to your partner in your personal vows or in a letter you might exchange with each other on your wedding day.

Available on Amazon!

Cover Photo: Victor Sizemore   vcsphoto.com

Made in the USA
Las Vegas, NV
11 April 2023

70457401R00046